WALTZ WITH ME

My Dancing Lessons with the King

Unlock Heaven's Glorious Realm of the Supernatural

PAULA DOUGLAS

Miracles happen to those who believe

xulon PRESS

www.xulonpress.com

DEDICATION

A thousand "THANKS" to the Holy Ghost and Momma for all of the teaching...
The seeds planted fell on good soil......

My heart overflows with a goodly theme, I address my psalm to a King. My tongue is like the pen of a ready writer.
-Psalms 45:1 (AMP)

TABLE OF CONTENTS

Chapter 1

The Waltz Begins....

"Eye hath not seen, nor ear heard, neither have entered into the heart of man, the things which God hath prepared for those that love him" (I Corinthians 2:9 KJV).

The sights and sounds of the room filled my senses. I could feel my heart beating fast with excitement. Vendors from around the world were displaying their goods. I pushed through the crowd as they handled the products. I began to question God as to what was I doing at the Christian Embassy in Jerusalem? Why had he sent me to the other side of the world to celebrate the Feast of Tabernacles? In the distance, way across the room, I saw a beautifully quilted jacket that was hanging for display. It caught my eye, and like any shopper worth her salt, I made a beeline for it. When I got to the table I began to look at all the quilted work this gifted lady had done. Why there were jackets and book covers and items too numerous to name, and then I saw the most beautifully quilted eyeglass pouch. It was magnificent all arrayed in vividly colored silk and handcrafted embroidered work. Whoosh, as I held the case in my hand, I was immediately reminded of a dream that God had given to me sometime back. I knew from that moment my life would forever be changed.

Now my life has never been ordinary. The doctors told momma that she would never have any more children after my brother was born. He had lay in the birth canal for three days, so long in fact that his head had begun to take on an oblong shape. Her body was in no condition to carry another child. But God, say **BUT GOD** somebody, had another plan. Four years later, at a little country church, out in the woods, as we Southerner's would say, momma met with God. Two Holy Ghost-filled, old-time prayer warriors lay her on the altar that night and prayed the prayer of faith. They prayed that she would conceive and bring forth an anointed child that would serve the Lord! Now this was against all natural odds because momma's womb was flipped over backwards and filled with fibroid tumors. Well, within six weeks, momma was pregnant with me. On many occasions she would tell me of my delivery and how she asked everyone to leave the room and let the Holy Ghost deliver her baby that she knew would be a little girl.

Once a baby girl, now a blossoming young woman in Jerusalem at the Christian Embassy, I stood and pondered.... was that really a dream? I'm not so sure it was that as much as a spiritual experience. It was so real and breathtaking that I could not share my experience with any one for some time. Tears would flow down my cheeks as I recalled that moment with God. Let me try to relay what I dreamed, what I experienced. I heard in the distance, the sound of an orchestra playing music from the turn of the century. I looked up ahead and saw a beautiful ballroom with a shining dance floor. Suddenly I was at the edge of the dance floor, dressed in a magnificent ball gown. Moving toward me was a man who was clothed in a white flowing garment. He had what appeared to be a gold rope tied around his waist. I could not see his face. It was as if light penetrated his garment from the inside out. To my amazement, out of all the people dancing on and standing to the side of the grand wooden floor, he chose me. I was awestruck that he wanted to dance with me, with me. I looked down and in my hand I held two quilted cases. I thought in my mind, "these will disqualify me from the dance. How could this be that the Lord of the dance was selecting me as a dance partner?" At that moment, the Master asked, *"Will you waltz with me?"* Gently, I slipped my hand, which held the two cases, into his and the waltz of a lifetime began.

A dream or an experience? Real, vivid, breath-taking... awesome, my time with the "Lord of the Dance"...... God.

Chapter 2

You Are Not The Violin!
Just the microphone....

I am the vine, ye are the branches: He that abideth in me,
and I in him, the same bringeth forth much fruit: for without
me ye can do nothing" (John 15:5 KJV).

It seems to reason, that humankind has one silk thread in
common. It's when you and I inhale a deep, cleansing
breath and ponder...what is this thing called "life" all about?
Well, that exact thought was the meditation of my heart as
I fell into a restful sleep. Now, isn't it puzzling to think of
those who are not mindful of God, yet they too ponder this
age-old question? My answer was revealed to me as I slept.

I appeared in a vast auditorium, stage left. An associate,
I immediately recognized, greeted me. He was taking me
on a tour of a facility that apparently I was steward over or
was about to be the steward of. We made our way down the
steps into the altar area, which we crossed to get to the other
side of the stage. There we saw the video production and
television command center. A team was diligently working
on editing media footage. It seemed as if they all knew me
by name. I felt this sudden flush of amazement because it

was as if I had been propelled into my own future! Everyone there was in the right moment of time but I was looking into my tomorrow with an overwhelming sense of God's clarion assignment for my life's work.

Instantly I felt alone and unaware of anyone around me. I found myself center stage, at the bottom of the steps, in a darkened auditorium. On the stage a dazzling bright spotlight suddenly flashed on. In the spotlight was a violin. This was no ordinary instrument, for this violin was extravagant in craftsmanship. The color was so vividly rich in tone. It was heavenly! I looked in amazement because it was horizontally suspended in mid-air. Nothing appeared to be holding it up. I reached to touch the violin and asked, "Should I play the violin?" Before I could touch the instrument, I heard this thunderous voice. It was as if this voice was echoing through a galaxy of time. This voice said to me, *"You are not the violin, you are but a microphone. You are to keep your instrument in working order so that as the music of the violin plays it can go through you and be magnified for the hearing of the people."*

I awoke with easiness in my spirit. For now I had an understanding of what Jesus meant when he spoke about the vine being the source from which the branches draw strength to bear fruit. The vine produces the life giving sap, which runs through the branches to produce nourishing fruit for the partakers. God, the violin, plays the melody that is magnified through the microphone, a yielded vessel, and pierces the heart of all men.

and the dance continues.........

Chapter 3

An Open Door of Destiny....

"I know thy works: behold, I have set before thee an open door, and no man can shut it:
(Revelation 3:8 KJV).

Now, some will probably say that forty-three years is a mighty long time of preparation. And I would have a tendency to agree. I was privileged to stand beside an awesome woman of God. At an early age I determined in my heart, to glean as much as I possibly could from her. For I knew that God had a plan for my life and that he had richly blessed me with an incredible spiritual heritage. But who knew that Momma's passing would thrust me so quickly into my *"open door of destiny?"* Destiny, for me was known as, the unforeseen opportunity to use all the knowledge that I had acquired about how God's kingdom operates. Since Momma's passing, I have learned that you cannot tell God how to illustrate or paint your life. For if you or I were allowed to do so, it would only pale in comparison to the beautiful sketches and colors he desires to portray. After all, He is the master artist.

I cannot remember a day going by that I didn't hear my momma praying in the Holy Ghost. Some say, she was born before her time. Things that many churches and people are just now experiencing in God, Momma taught forty years ago. I grew up praising and worshipping God in the dance, believing in divine healing, praying and singing in a heavenly language and by faith, speaking things into existence that were not. I was taught to believe that a lively and intimate relationship with God is available to everyone who desires it. Yes, I guess you could say, Momma was definitely a forerunner of that heavenly glory realm many are just now experiencing.

Destiny, your foreordained appointment with God. It is an open door for which you were birthed on earth to walk through. When you reach your moment in time with God, you will have been equipped, cultivated, matured, and prepared for the assignment. The day destiny knocks, you must answer, "Yes Lord, here I am, send me."

Well, He called and I answered. One day I was a twenty-year veteran schoolteacher with a master's degree in educational leadership and the next I was responsible for leading a congregation of believers. But like Moses and his burning bush experience, where God guides He provides! Little did I know how beautifully the master could couple my spiritual teaching with my natural training. These two elements, like wind and fire collided. What was produced was a small packaged powerhouse for God who made an entrance onto the dance floor that would sweep through the nations.

Limitations...there are none when you know who you are in Christ. You are positioned in Him and an open door of destiny awaits.

and the dance continues.......

Chapter 4

Dance Lesson # 1. "You Gotta Get Your Praise On"....

"Enter into His gates with thanksgiving, and into His courts with praise: be thankful unto Him, and bless His name" (Psalm 100:4 KJV).

The path of thanksgiving, praise, and worship leads to God's manifested glory. Think about what an awesome statement that is. The manifested presence of God who created the universe comes and surrounds you like a father's strong, loving arms, encourages you like a mother's gentle touch, and excites you like a lover's passionate kiss. He desires for every believer to journey this path and find Him waiting with open arms.

My heart still leaps with excitement every time I go to the house of the Lord! You see, growing up that was what we did. We were either at the house of the Lord, or people were gathered at our home for a cottage meeting. My family did not seek entertainment through a visiting social event, some new restaurant, or the latest movie. We went to the house of the Lord and spent our time in His presence. Those are some of the best memories that I have of my childhood. I enjoyed hearing and seeing the worshipers "get blessed," as we called it. Why sometimes it could be quite entertaining, especially to some little ones that were watching with eyes wide open. But those times taught me what true worship is, for you see Jesus said to the woman at the well, *"the hour cometh, and now is, when the true worshipers shall worship the Father in spirit and in truth: for the Father seeketh such to worship him" (John 4:23).* Oh, how the Lord desires to meet us through true worship. The Holy Spirit is an awesome teacher. Just ask Him to lead and guide you into all truth and He will.

I liken this journey of "true worship" unto a mountain trek. King David asked in Psalm 24:3 *"who shall ascend into the hill of the Lord? Or who shall stand in his holy place?"* Our desired destination is the mountaintop. The foot of the mountain is okay but it isn't the top of the peak where the air is clear, the sky seems bluer, and the atmosphere is lighter. Along this mountain trek to true worship, one will encounter a steep climb. The fainthearted climbers quickly turn back and are easily satisfied with the two-mile hike and head for camp. But to the true worshipers who worship in spirit and truth that is not the ending of our worship experience. It is but the beginning of an intimate relationship with the Lord God Almighty. We are looking for an encounter with a living God who is able to touch us in a tangible way.

Hiking a mountain requires the appropriate gear. A ballerina's tutu is not sufficient for such a trek. A well-prepared hiker will have the right clothes, food and equipment for the task at hand. I remember one summer our family went on vacation to Hawaii. One particular day, my Dad decided that we were going to drive to the top of the mountain and get a bird's eye view of the city. I still get a little rush of excitement thinking about that family outing. God blessed me with such wonderful parents that love Him with their whole heart. While we were traveling around the coast, shorts and a t-shirt were fine but as soon as we began to increase our altitude and climb the mountain, the air temperature changed drastically! When we got out of the car to see the view it was freezing cold! A heavy jacket was needed to be able to stand outside and pleasurably enjoy the beauty of the Hawaiian island seascape. I was not prepared for the drastic temperature drop. My viewing experience was a quick one because I was not properly equipped for the journey. Likewise, we as worshipers must be prepared when *"the Spirit and the bride say, Come" (Revelation 22:17).*

Thanksgiving is at the foot of the mountain. It is a mindset that we must possess, a condition of the heart. By that I mean we should continuously be thankful to God for all that He has done for us. Thankfulness should be a part of our constant thought process. It should be second nature to us. Words of appreciation and gratitude toward God should be bubbling up in the believer's spirit at all times. Apostle Paul wrote in Ephesians 5:20, that believers should be *"giving thanks always for all things unto God and the Father in the name of our Lord Jesus Christ."* David declares in Psalm 119:62, *"At midnight I will rise to give thanks unto thee because of thy righteous judgments."*

Thanksgiving can be defined as an expression of gratitude. It is an appreciation for a kindness received, an attitude of the heart. Matthew 12:34 states that, *"out of the abundance of the heart the mouth speaketh."* It can be seen in the natural realm as well as the spiritual. Think about the pessimist versus the optimist. Out of the mouth or heart of the pessimist will flow doom and gloom. From the optimist you will hear words of victory and accomplishment. What is in your heart will come out through your mouth. We must fill our spirit with the words of life and what the word says about our situation and circumstances. Thanksgiving truly is a heart condition. It is a heart filled with adoration toward a loving God who has *"shared our weaknesses and was touched with the feelings of our infirmities"* (Hebrews 4:15).

After leaving the foot of the mountain, those that are hungry for more of God begin the ascent (upward climb) into praise. Praise is the demonstrative aspect of true worship. It can be defined as the outward expression of approval or admiration. If there is one that we truly approve of it is our Lord and Savior Jesus Christ.

King David flowed in this affectionate outpouring toward his God. What "a praiser" he was. He knew the pathway to enter in and touch the Father's heart. He also understood that it was a continual state of being. He declares in Psalm 34:1, *"I will bless the Lord at all times; his praise shall continually be in my mouth."* It was from this book that I learned to forever flow in praise. This meditation of the heart, which spills out through the mouth, will position you in the love of Christ where no one or circumstance can touch you. You literally become cloaked in and enveloped by His praise. Isaiah 61:3 describes it as, *"exchanging or slipping off the spirit of heaviness for the garment of praise."*

There was a time that I was concerned about how "people" would receive my expression of praise. I knew that I was praising Him with my whole heart as David did when he brought the Ark of the Covenant to Jerusalem. We find in II Samuel 6:20, Michal, David's wife ridiculed him for the praise he gave God. I knew that if I could lose my inhibitions through dancing before the Lord with all my might as David did, then my Godly sphere of influence would increase so that I could spiritually feed a nation. One night as I was preparing for bed, I asked God for a revelation on the matter.

I dreamed that there was a magnificently appointed chair on which a King sat. I very pleasingly went over and sat in the King's lap. This was no ordinary King, for he cheerfully welcomed the attention. I was impressed by the fact that there was so much joy coming from this King's very being.

Why one could not help but to begin to smile, laugh, and rejoice over how great this King was. He quickly discerned that I had a question for him. So feeling completely at ease, I shared with him my concerns about what others thought of my expression of praise and worship towards him. He so lovingly looked me in the eye and said, *"whatever the King wants is what the King will have because the King has dominion over all the domain."* Instantly, all of my fear was relieved! And in its place was an assurance that I personally had found an approving favor in the eyes of the King.

So the celebration of praise begins. It is a joyful event to celebrate the "goodness" of the Lord and to bring down the strongholds of the enemy. David declares in Psalm 30:11 that, *"Thou hast turned for me my mourning into dancing: thou hast put off my sackcloth, and girded me with gladness."*

Praise is also a powerful weapon of spiritual war! I have never encountered a situation or circumstance yet that praise couldn't defeat or take me out of. Praise will change the very atmosphere that surrounds you. Jehoshaphat obeyed the word of the Lord in II Chronicles 20:15 when Jahaziel prophesied, *"Be not afraid nor dismayed by reason of this great multitude; for the battle is not yours, but God's."* Verse 21-22 declares that Jehoshaphat, *"appointed singers unto the Lord, and that should praise the beauty of holiness, as they went out before the army, and to say, Praise the Lord; for his mercy endureth forever. And when they began to sing and to praise, the Lord set ambushments against the children of Ammon, Moab, and Mount Seir."* Praise will cut a pathway out of trouble every single time!

But this extravagant explosion of "adoration, joy and war" only takes us half way up the mountain. The top of the peak is where our spirit desires to commune with the living God. The top of the mountain is where worship, in the purest sense, begins to take place. Up until this point, only an external, soulish experience has been encountered. The ascending mountain trek now begins to plateau out into a high place of peace, calmness, and serenity. Remember, we are a spirit that is having an earthly experience!

You may ask, how long does it take one, on this mountain climbing experience, to reach the top? Must one go through this process every time one desires to commune with God? Both are great questions that have no definite answer. For our relationship with God is just that, a relationship. I cannot answer how long it will take you to align your heart with His. I do not know your heart condition at any given moment. I do not know the battles that you are currently waging. I do not know how much fear is on the inside of you concerning an intimate time of fellowship with your creator. These questions can only be answered when you begin the mountain's ascent. For those of us who continually climb the mountain, intimacy is always close at hand.

Solomon, in the Song of Songs, describes the intimacy of pure worship so well. The bride begins this song with... "Let him kiss me with the kisses of his mouth: for thy love is better than wine. Because of the savor of thy good ointment thy name is as ointment poured forth, therefore do the virgins love thee. Draw me, we will run after thee: the King hath brought me into chambers: we will be glad and rejoice in thee, we will remember thy love more than wine: the upright love thee." Worship is so beautiful because you realize it is then that you are looking full in the face of God. Sometimes there are no words to express the euphoria you are overcome with. There are times when tears flow and they become the words of your heart. Peace, gentleness, and unconditional love begin to saturate your very soul. It is like no other experience on earth because it is not earthly; it is heavenly. There is no fear in this intimacy. Never do you have to be afraid of exposing yourself to such a loving creator. He fashioned you just as you are. Imperfections are nonexistent, shortcomings are not noticed, and you know without a word being spoken how your expressions of love please him. It truly is a heart thing. Two hearts begin to beat as one. Each heart signals and then aligns into one beating rhythm. Minutes may lead into hours but never shall one come away from a time of true intimate worship the same as they entered in. The Father exposes His heart to the believer and the believer becomes saturated with the very mind of Christ. You know His will and desires for you without even asking. It is true communication, spirit to spirit.

Staying in worship ushers you into the "Glory Realm." Standing in His presence exposes you to the eternal. It is when God comes into your realm of reality. I often sing the song,

I feel Jesus,
I feel Jesus,
I feel Jesus, Jesus, Jesus,
In this place,
How my soul does
Burn within me,
For I feel Jesus,
He's in.... my reality.

The truth of the matter is we enter His realm of the Heavenly. The Glory of the Lord is not from this earthly realm. It is from Heaven's realm. It is the manifestation of His presence that is revealed to us. Apostle Paul summed it up well in II Corinthians 3:17-18 when he stated that, *"the Lord is that Spirit: and where the Spirit of the Lord is, there is liberty. But we all, with open face beholding as in a glass the glory of the Lord, are changed into the same image from glory to glory, even as by the Spirit of the Lord."*

At our church, we have a "Glory Outpouring." It is not church as usual! There is not an agenda, just time allowed for believers to come and worship until the glory appears. I have learned that you must produce the right atmosphere that is conducive for the Holy Spirit to have His way. He does as He pleases. We must follow Him. I have found that lively music and songs, at first, will bring the people into an attitude of unity. We clap our hands and shout unto the Lord and tell Him of His goodness. When we get our hearts and minds on the things of the Lord, the cares of life quickly fade away. Those that have a heart of thanksgiving, of truly being grateful for the things that He has done on their behalf, seem to flow the easiest. When unity is evident among the people we then move the songs into a slower pace where we can praise Him for all the great things He has done. Praise gives way to an atmosphere of worship every time. When the spirit of worship comes into the house, believers become gentle in their demonstration; even if flying a banner. It is the most beautiful thing to see worship come into the sanctuary. At some point, you will forget everyone around you. You become so lost in Him that you are unaware of anyone else. Some cry, some stand in awe, while others lay prostrate before Him. The spirit of revelation comes to His people during these times of glory. I identify it with Revelation Chapter 4. I call it "The Throne Room Experience." It is where the four and twenty elders fall down before him, casting their crowns at His feet and say, *"Thou art worthy, O Lord to receive glory and honor and power: for thou hast created all things, and for thy pleasures they are and were created."* When the spirit of revelation comes, different manifestations take place. I have witnessed people being instantly healed. I have even seen what appears to be a white smoke fill the room. People have seen bright lights with gold and blue stars sparkling. What always amazes me the most is the ease that the "glory" (His Presence) of God brings. There is no stress, strain, or struggle with it. You have a knowing of what God is doing. You have a confidence in Him as never before. It is as if God has opened your eyes of understanding to His method of operation. The glory realm is awesome and inspiring. Once you have tasted of it, nothing else will ever satisfy you again.

Once I became curious as to how God receives our worship. I knew how it was flowing out of my inner most being; like a river towards Him. But I wondered; how was He receiving it? The meditation of my heart was soon answered in a night vision. In this vision, I was suspended in time among beautifully hung stars. Above me I could sense the vastness of God himself. Below me I could see the earth in all of its fullness. The stars were shining ever so brightly. And there I was; suspended motionless in His creation we call the universe. The question once again entered my mind; how does God receive the glory of our praise and worship? And just like that, I saw the most brilliant light beams begin to shine forth from the earth heavenward. My soul leaped with joy at the expression of worship I was seeing. Why, praise and worship as perfect white light was being beamed straight into the heavens. There to be received by God, our creator, who recognized it as pure love his creation has for Him. Now I could clearly understand the prophet Isaiah when he said, *"Arise, shine; for the light has come, and the glory of the Lord is risen upon thee"* (Isaiah 61:1).

Oh, the awesomeness of the peak of the mountain! If we could only stay there. Going there daily is what fuels and enables the believer to accomplish the God given assignment in their life. Jesus himself always drew aside to pray and commune with the Father. He did the works of the Father through the power of the Holy Spirit. He has now commissioned us to do not only these works but also greater works than these.

The mountain trek is easily accomplished with the right gear. The path to becoming a true worshiper is guided by the hands of a loving savior and friend. This mountain climb begins in our heart of thanksgiving; which explodes in a praise of adoration. Our praise provides the right atmosphere and environment for worship. Worship then suspends us in the glory realm of His presence where the supernatural can flow.

the dance lesson continues.......

Chapter 5

Dance Lesson # 2.
Forgiveness, "me first Lord".....

"And when ye stand praying, forgive, if ye have aught against any: that your Father also which is in heaven may forgive you your trespasses" ~ Jesus ~ (Mark 11:25 KJV).

Forgiveness is a miraculous healing agent. In chemistry we can compare it to a chemical agent. The agent is what has the power to cause change. For example, when two chemicals are combined, if one is a change agent, then the result of the combination of two chemicals will be a newly formed substance. As believers, we can apply that same principle to healing. Our sick or infirmed body is like the basic chemical in a scientific equation. When we apply a change agent, in this case forgiveness, to any and every situation in our life then the ending result will be a manifested healing in our natural body.

I was in a service at All Nations Church with Pastors Bonnie and Mahesh Chavda. The speaker for the conference was Bill Johnson. He was talking about what God was doing in his church in Redding, California. He told how God was using ordinary people to lay hands on the sick and how they recover. After speaking for a while he began to call out healings that were manifesting among the people. He asked those that had pain in their neck to stand and receive their healing. He paused and asked believers that were close by to gently lay their hand on the sick and pray for the manifestation of healing to come. There was an elderly lady standing in the row in front of me. So I did as he asked. I placed my hand on her shoulder and prayed that God would heal her painful neck. As we were praying, Bill Johnson said, "God wants to heal all those that have been in car accidents and have been left with pain in their body." He began by explaining that the "lord of the flies" is drawn to dead things. He related to us that the area of pain in our body was a place where death could settle and that unforgiveness gave sickness a place to be housed. He asked us to simply put our hand on the place of pain and forgive the one that had caused the car accident, even if we had to forgive ourselves.

Now I had been in three car accidents in the past ten years. Once a lady ran a red light and smashed into the rear driver's side. Twice I was rear ended in morning traffic by those anxious to get to work. Each time the doctor's report was the same. I had been left with a twelve percent disability in my back just between the shoulder blades due to three whiplashes. The pain was always there. No matter how often I visited the chiropractor for treatment over the years, I was always aware of the injuries. I began to shrug my shoulders to find a place of comfort. For several years I had grown accustomed to not standing up straight.

I desired my healing to manifest but I never realized or acknowledged that I had not forgiven those that caused the accidents that resulted in my constant pain. As instructed, I began to go through each accident in my mind. As I did, I began to forgive person one, two, and then three. As I was forgiving the third person I felt a soft sensation between my shoulders. The only way I can explain it is that it was like my granny's big, fluffy white powder puff. On her dressing table was a beautiful white oyster shell container that housed a sweet scented powder. As a child, I remember simply taking the puff and gently running it across my face. How comforting it was. It smelled like my grandmother and was as gentle as she was. What comfort! Well, that is what I felt during the healing service that day in Charlotte, NC. I felt Granny's powder puff being gently dabbed three times against my naked skin. I know now that it was the gentle healing power of Jesus that manifested when I chose to forgive others from my heart. When my heart was clean and pure, the pain left and I was able to straighten my shoulders. My healing manifested when I chose to no longer carry unforgiveness.

The intent of a one's heart can be unknown and hidden. Jeremiah 17:9 says, *"the heart is deceitful above all things, and desperately wicked: who can know it?"*

No one can reveal the intent of the heart but God. Verse 10 clearly confirms this by stating that, *"I the Lord search the heart. I try the reins (the emotions), even to give every man according to his ways, and according to the fruit of his doing."* I challenge you as I was challenged that day in Bill Johnson's service. Choose to forgive those that "despitefully use you" (Matt. 5:44) and in your act of forgiveness you *"heap coals of fire upon their head"* (Rom. 12:20). You will be benefited by this forgiveness because healing comes to our broken bodies through deliberate acts of kindness.

Forgiveness truly is a change agent. Meditate these following scriptures and watch the power of forgiveness unfold in your life.

"if ye forgive men their trespasses, your heavenly Father will also forgive you."

Jesus ~ Matt. 6:14

"Judge not, and ye shall not be judged: condemn not, and ye shall not be condemned: forgive, and ye shall be forgiven: Give, and it shall be given unto you: good measure, pressed down, and shaken together, and running over, shall men give into your bosom. For with the same measure that ye mete withal it shall be measured to you again."

Jesus ~ Luke 6:37-38

"and be ye kind to one another, tenderhearted, forgiving one another, even as God for Christ's sake hath forgiven you."

Apostle Paul to the Ephesians 4:32

the dance lesson continues......

Chapter 6

Dance Lesson # 3.
Help! Renew My Mind God,
"for we have the mind
of Christ"...

"If there be therefore any consolation in Christ, if any comfort of love, if any fellowship of the Spirit, if any bowels and mercies, Fulfill ye my joy, that ye be likeminded, having the same love, being of one accord, of one mind. Let this mind be in you, which was also in Christ Jesus" (Philippians 2:1-2,5 KJV).

God's Kingdom mindset equals risk; it's the trust factor. In direct opposition there is the natural mindset, which operates within the boundaries of reasoning. Conforming to carnal, natural reasoning sets limitations on a mighty God who is capable of doing mighty acts and deeds. Total trust, in a miracle working God, will result in the things which seem impossible coming into the realm of possibility. As believers, we must allow the Holy Spirit to transform our minds by the washing of water by the word (Ephesians 5:26).

Luke chapter one and two provides us with a bird's eye-view of this principle in action. We find the Virgin Mary and the Priest Zechariah. Both were apparently minding their own business by fulfilling their required obligations and duties. But then the supernatural invaded the natural and an angel of the Lord shows up. Hmmm, what is one to do when an angel of the Lord shows up and speaks? Something must give. Carnal reasoning must bow to a transformed mind that is capable of receiving the things of the Spirit. Your spirit man becomes energized and your natural man becomes weak in the knees.

The trust factor, which is God's mindset, apparently was not working for Zechariah that day. The angel appeared and said, *" fear not, for thy prayer is heard."* Zechariah's response was, *"how shall I know this?"* The angel then identified himself as Gabriel who stands in the presence of God and told him that he was sent with this message of good tidings. The question posed by Zechariah was filled with carnal reasoning that resulted in a tied tongue until the announced child was born. Bummer, what a sad, long nine months that was for Zech.

Then we have the Virgin, named Mary. Such a simple little girl she was that day. Then the angel of the Lord showed up, as he did to Zechariah, and her life was forever changed. Carnal reasoning; no. Unwavering trust in a living God who invaded her realm of logic; yes. Given the magnitude of the message the angel was delivering that day, Mary received his words beautifully. Mary, said the angel, *"you shall conceive in your womb and bring forth a son and you shall call his name Jesus, the Son of God."* Her response was through a mind that did not try to process the things of God in a logical manner. She went into "free fall," fell into God's loving arms and said, *" be it unto me according to thy word."*

What a difference there is between a heavenly renewed mind and an earthly fixed, logical mind. Jesus operated outside of natural reasoning where there were no boundaries or limitations to what the Spirit of God could and would do in this earthly realm. The only time He was limited was when unbelief was present. Unbelief is a killer to the things of the spirit. It is actually faith in the thing you fear coming to pass. The faith of God speaks that all things are possible to those that believe.

Our job, as believers, is to capture and subdue our natural way of thinking and replace that which has been captured with the thoughts and ways of God which are higher than ours. Romans 12:1-2 clearly defines our role as believers when Paul said, *"I beseech you therefore, brethren, by the mercies of God, that ye present your bodies a living sacrifice, holy, acceptable unto God, which is your reasonable service. And be not <u>conformed to this world</u>; but be ye <u>transformed by the renewing of your mind</u>, that ye may prove what is that good, and acceptable, and perfect, will of God."*

So the question arises, how do I believe, trust, and operate with a renewed mind?

Transforming truth #1, you must fill yourself with the Word of God. You must consume it both day and night. You must meditate on it continually like food that your digestive system is processing for nutrition.

The Word of God is good news. It is the motivating factor that can never lead you astray. The good news must be rehearsed over and over in your mind. For every action there is an equal and opposite reaction. Every time the enemy sends you a negative thought, you counteract it with the positive Word of God. Bad circumstances may come your way but a mind that has stayed on the Word of God will combat the darkness with the light and win every single time. When you know what God says about your situation, you will always come through the difficulties successfully.

According to Deuteronomy chapter 28, as believers, we are blessed when we are obedient to His Word. We are to be the head and not the tail, the lender and not the borrower. We are blessed in the city and in the field. But what happens when your checkbook doesn't reflect that belief? You know when there is no one in front of all those zeros. It just says zero! You will live a life of defeat if you begin to believe that balance and allow lack to become your mindset instead of what the Word says about your financial situation.

The Word of God must be the final authority in our lives. I can remember a not so long ago time in my life that I needed God to intervene in my health. I had been given a bad report on my yearly mammogram. The doctors had retested me several times. All the results were the same. There was a lump in my breast. As a preliminary to having a biopsy, they sent me to have a film made at the teaching hospital that used the latest technology. Between my scheduled visits was a period of twenty-one days. I chose to turn to the Word of God as the final authority in my life. I renewed my mind daily in the Word as I fasted for the twenty-one days between my appointments. I presented *"my body as a living sacrifice"* and refused to be conformed to this world's report but was *"transformed by the renewing of my mind"* to God's way of thinking. Healing and atonement are clearly found in the suffering on the cross of our dear Lord and Savior, Jesus Christ. As Isaiah the prophet spoke in chapter 53 and verse 5, *"but he was wounded for our transgressions, he was bruised for our iniquities; the chastisement of our peace was upon him; and with his stripes we are healed."* I found the nourishment I needed to feed my mind so that my spirit could influence my soul into aligning with the success that God had appointed for me to walk in.

As I waited for the doctor to read my test film, I felt assured that "all is well." Not once did I set my eyes on what the report told me but my eyes were fixed on what God's Word said about my situation and circumstance. You see, this medical office was a sad place to be because not many received a positive report here. The nurses were solemn, very gentle and comforting, as if mourning with you about the medical need. I did not see any smiles or hear joyous laughing, just seriousness about the moment. Thank God He did not see the situation the way they saw it. It was to the nurse's surprise and my confirmation that the doctor entered the room and said, "I don't know why you are here, your films are normal, see your doctor next year for a regular check up." The Word of God truly was the final authority in my situation that day. And His Word can renew your mind also if you will but daily consume it as you do natural food for living.

Transforming truth #2, you must turn off all the externals in your life. Turning off the outside, externals that bombard your life is key to your success in obtaining a renewed mind. You may say to me, Paula what do you mean by externals of life? Let me share with you what I call the "distractions of life." These distractions are things that stimulate you from the outside in. External factors are all of the sights and sounds that fill your five senses such as but not limited to television, newspapers, phone calls, internet, or hanging out with friends. This is but a small list of the externals that stimulate your life. These motivating factors speak into your life subconsciously. What you surround yourself with, you become. As a simple example let's say you hang around someone who is down and sad for just a few minutes. It would not be surprising to you that before long you are sad also. The same would be true when you spend time with someone that is happy and filled with joy. Just like that, before you know it you will be laughing and expressing happiness just as they are.

The year 2007 was a great year for fasting in my life. Then again 2008 was also a great year of fasting in my life. Even though God designated these two years as a time of fasting in my life, they were packaged quite differently. 2007 was a year of food fasting for me. By God's mercy and strength I was able to complete a forty-day water fast. I was down to a mere ninety-five pounds and had many people joining with me in prayer that God would sustain my life and hold me up during this time of dedication. 2008 was a different fast for me. For the complete year God had me fast all the externals of my life and seek him only. By the externals of life I mean that God had me lay aside television, all books (religious as well), magazines, cds, dvds, the radio, the telephone (only as necessary), shopping, eating in restaurants, hobbies, and any and everything that would "distract" me from Him. For one solid year I stayed on my face before Him reading His Word, praying, fasting and only ministering at my appointed church times, corporate prayer meetings, and conferences He lead me to speak in. All the external things in life that caused me to shift my eyes from Him were removed by His loving hand because He desired to spend time with me. The Holy Spirit alone through the Word of God influenced my way of thinking, changed my ability to meditate and wait on Him, and stirred up my passionate love for the things of God as never before.

My mind had to be uncluttered with the things of life so that He could fill my mind, through His Holy Word, with His way of thinking and doing things. What a delight to have the mind of Christ operating in us daily so that we can live this life successfully just as He has ordained.

Transforming truth #3, you must replay all the great things God has done for you. It has been noted by psychologist that any given person on any given day will have one repetitive thought that the mind will repeat some six hundred times in a day. For instance, everyone can recall to mind a catchy commercial jingle that has stuck with you over the years. That's why the commercial industry attaches a jingle to a product. Unknowingly you will be reminded to purchase their product when you think of the tune. Also our media industry has also learned to attach a product to a spokesperson. We sometimes purchase a product because a celebrity has promoted it or has been seen using it. Now, take the way the brain works and couple that with someone who is experiencing fear, defeat, anxiety, and any other negative emotion. The down and out person almost without knowing it is talking themselves into depression and despair. If this is true of the unrenewed mind, doesn't it stand to reason that the mind that has been filled with memories of what God has done will counteract the world's negative impact on the believer? Replaying what God has done in your life, how He has answered your prayers, saved you from destruction, made a way where there seemed to be no way, turned your ashes into beauty, picked you up out of the ditch, moved you to the front of the line, gave you the promotion, favored you above others more qualified, and wants to be in every decision you make in life, should dominate your thinking daily.

Stinking thinking is a killer! Replaying the negative aspects of any situation can have detrimental results. Proverbs 23:7 clearly tells us, *"for as he thinketh in his heart, so is he."* You must clean up your thinking through the Word of God.

I have a tried and true method that keeps me replaying the great things God has done in my life. If you are convinced that what your eye and ear gate picks up does not affect you then the next time you go to the theater to view a movie try this. Purchase your ticket and proceed directly to where the movie is being shown. Do not stop by the concession stand. Find your seat and enjoy the previews of upcoming events. Just as you are starting to enjoy the trailers, a commercial for popcorn and soda will come on the screen. The next thing you are aware of is the line you are in to purchase the promoted food. Point proved!

So how do I put the accomplishments of the Lord in my life ever before me....I journal! I keep a daily journal of all the things God did in me, through me, and with me on any given day. Some days it may be just a one liner, other days may be a page or more. Now Isaiah 59:19 declares that, *"When the enemy shall come in like a flood, the spirit of the Lord shall lift up a standard against him"* for my benefit. So when discouragement or any other negative emotion or thought tries to bombard my mind, I open my journal and read aloud the good things God has done. As quickly as the enemy came, he will retreat because James 4:7 says, *"Resist the devil, and he will flee from you."* Negative, toxic emotions (the enemy's lies), will not remain when you remind yourself of the good things that have taken place in your life because of God.

Transforming truth #4, you must expect the supernatural to be common-place in your life. God is a supernatural God. He is not spooky or scary but He can circumvent natural circumstances and situations so that you prosper in all your ways. Allowing the river of the supernatural to flow through you should become a way of life and feel natural. Miracles should be popping up all around you, everyday! When there is a need in your life, with expectation that God is going to supernaturally move for you, your faith should be actively pursuing God's answer. It does not matter if you were born on the right side of the tracks, have the proper education, or know the right people to get God to intervene in your life. He desires to make a way for you where there is no natural avenue of success available to you. This way He alone will get all the glory for the great things that are accomplished in and through your life.

I find an interesting story, which documents a supernatural intervention, in the 12th chapter of the book of Acts. Now this story is interesting because the people portrayed so long ago are much like the people of today; stunned by answered prayer. It was especially confounding because an angel had been sent by God to visibly escort Peter out of difficulty. Let me explain. Recorded in Acts we find the Apostle

Peter, because of preaching the gospel, has been chained up in Herod's jail awaiting punishment until after Easter. This small space in time allowed for the church to pray for his release *"without ceasing" (verse 5)*.

As a sidebar, you and I should extract wisdom from this event. The early church's method of practice was to not stop praying until the desired results came! Today we, as believers, sometimes give up far too quickly before we actually give God an opportunity to produce tangible results in our own situations. Supernatural intervention can and does yield amazing results. Results not for the faint-hearted but results for those that, with tenacity, refuse to let go of the promises of God. Astonishing results for those that dare to believe God and that He will do what He says He will do even in the face of opposition. Now that is expecting the supernatural to invade the natural and yield results that can benefit every believer.

But back to Peter who was in jail, sleeping between two soldiers, bounds with two chains, way down in the second jail behind a locked gate. There was no natural way for Peter to be freed from the current situation. This dilemma found him waiting for Herod's decision. This decision would have Peter executed the day after the religious feast. How many can see that this situation was not working for Peter's good? Jailed for preaching the gospel: awaiting execution because it pleased the people. Not good! But then the believers were praying for God to intervene on his behalf. And, whamo it happened... freed by an angel and knocking at the door. Results for the faint-hearted? I don't think so. Astonishing results for those that dare to believe...I know so!

What an example of an awesome God. One who is working supernaturally in this world to benefit the believers just like you and me. We must pursue the God who helped Apostle Peter that day. The miracle working God who is still alive and powerful today...his name, Jesus!

So, renewal of the mind comes when the Word of God is our ultimate authority. Consume it daily and think like God thinks. Turn off the business of life and let the life of Christ flow through you. When daily life with all of its difficulties arises; remember what the Lord has already brought you through and the hurdles you have crossed. The anthem for all believers is to.... expect the supernatural as though it were natural!

the dance lesson continues......

Chapter 7

Dance Lesson # 4.
Jesus, "the name of all authority"…

"Wherefore God also hath highly exalted him, and given him <u>a name which is above</u> <u>every name</u>: that <u>at the name of Jesus every knee shall bow</u>, of things in heaven, and things in earth, and things under the earth; and that every tongue should confess that Jesus Christ is Lord, to the glory of God the Father" (Philippians 2:9-11 KJV).

What a comforting scripture. We as believers have been given the key to all authority: the name of Jesus Christ. The question is, will we use the authority that we have been given or will we try to be successful in our own name or strength? I am not sure about the authority of your name but the authority of my name is less than the weight of a bird's feather. And a small bird at best! My name doesn't have much clout to go with it. No maître d' gives me the best table, no valet wants to drive my car, and no product sells because my name is attached to it. My name, quite frankly, is worthless. But let's not confuse my name, and its lack of value, with the name that is far more powerful than any other word in heaven or in earth; the name of Jesus.

What could make this name, the name of Jesus so different than any other name? To answer this question we must exam the one who gave this name and declared it **the name** above all other names. Matthew, the tax collector, in chapter 1 verse 23 repeats the prophet Isaiah when he writes, *"behold, a virgin shall be with child, and shall bring forth a son, and they shall call his name Immanuel, which being interpreted is, God with us."* The angel told Joseph in a dream that Mary, his betrothed wife, would bring forth a son who should be named Jesus; he would save his people from their sins (verse 21). So who would have this authority to send the Holy Ghost to overshadow a chosen virgin that she should carry the messiah who would reign over the house of Jacob and of his kingdom there should be no end? Clearly the Bible reveals to us that God himself sent His messenger, Gabriel, to proclaim the good news. Gabriel states in verse 31 of this same chapter that Mary would conceive in her womb, and bring forth a son, and His name shall be called Jesus.

A messenger sent from God to invade man's natural mental capabilities! Oh how delightful! God tending to His business, via the supernatural which defies the realm of carnal reasoning.

So here we have the messiah, named Jesus by God, planted in the womb of a virgin. How awesome! Try to wrap your mind around that. It may leave you speechless to say the least. But the biblical text clearly directs our attention to God when contemplating the value of this name: the name of Jesus.

Jesus once again gets an approval from his heavenly Father the day He is baptized in the river Jordan by his cousin, John. Luke documents the event by telling us that *"Jesus also being baptized, and praying, the heaven opened, and the Holy Ghost descended in a bodily shape like a dove upon him, and a voice came from heaven, which said, Thou art my beloved Son; in thee I am well pleased"* (Luke 3:21-22). It is undeniable that God found pleasure in sending His son to this earth. Our minds wonder why would the God of all creation do such a thing as this? Why would He even take notice of His creation and care enough for it to send His only son? This event at the river Jordan, definitively commissions Jesus, by God, to carry out His ordained plan for humankind. And what a great day that was for you and me when God publicly acknowledged His son for the greater work that was ahead.

God named and God approved; that was Jesus. After the wilderness of temptation, we now see him about the Father's business: teaching, preaching and healing all that were sick and diseased. Disciples followed him and learned of his ways, the hungry multitudes listened and were fed, the hopeless demoniacs were made free, and the sinful were forgiven of yesterday. The miraculous was commonplace in the life of Jesus. Who could resist His teaching that was with such authority? Who could surpass His compassion for the masses? Who could exceed this one who called life back to those that were dead? No one.... but Jesus-God named and God ordained.

No one took his life, He gave it willingly. Willingly He gave his life that you and I might have life and the life that He gives is the more abundant life, according to John 10:10. God has a great plan for you and me. He gave His son who modeled for us the behavior that He desires. For this abundant life, which is our desired outcome, we must follow God's kingdom method of operation. I desired to understand this successful life that John promises us, so I asked God to reveal to me His way so that I might follow His will and see a life of godly abundance. Not a life that is up one day and down the next. Not one that is lacking in His promises. Not a person who claims to be a believer but sees no signs of evidence that God is real or awake. So in my simple, elementary mind, God revealed to me his way of abundance. Simply put it is all in Jesus. Let me relate what I saw. I saw a multitude of foreign people sitting on the ground. They were waiting on me to minister to them. I prayed and said, "Heavenly Father, what do I do? I can't meet these people at their point of need. I don't have the right words to heal their broken hearts. I can't make miracles flow and mend their broken bodies nor am I the savior of their souls. What do I do?" Suddenly Jesus came. He said, "*put your hand in mine*". I stretched and reached my right hand out and put it in His left hand. As I did, He stretched His right hand out toward the people. He looked back at me and smiled the biggest smile I have ever seen. Then He looked back at the people and to my amazement, they were receiving miraculous healings, restoration and salvation. Wow, God made His kingdom way clear to me with that visitation. It's not us that does all the cool supernatural stuff, it's Jesus and we must have our hand in His so that He can do the work through us and get it to the ones in need. Now this scripture has new meaning for me. *"And these signs shall follow them that believe; in my name shall they cast out devils; they shall speak with new tongues; They shall take up serpents; and if they drink any deadly thing, it shall not hurt them; they shall lay hands on the sick, and they shall recover" (Mark 16: 17-18)*. The name of Jesus has been given to all believers. It is the ultimate and final authority over all of life's situations, circumstances, bodily sickness and disease. The name of Jesus causes darkness to flee, finances to flow, and beauty to trade places with ashes. Just use it!

Now that we have an understanding of the power of the name of Jesus, the question arises as to how the power of His name reaches us today? And once again my human logic is so simple that God had to reveal it to me in a night vision. I love the way God explains or reveals himself to us with graphics. I need the pictures, don't you? I am by no means a scientist, so one must excuse my lack of scientific jargon. Simply put, I saw a beam of white light extending from heaven to earth. The white light was filled with darkness that houses the entire universe, as we know it. There was tremendously fast movement within the tube or beam of light. The movement was leaving heaven and going to earth. When I saw this picture, my mind was stunned but my spirit began to clarify what I was looking at. Our Father God, in heaven, was extending a beam of light from his throne and touching earth. The shaft of light was the Holy Spirit. He was the conduit of travel for the power of the name of Jesus to flow from heaven to earth. As Jesus touched the earth by the conduit of the Holy Spirit, people's lives were forever being changed. And that is my limited understanding of how the name of Jesus enables us the believers to do exploits!

But you know me, the practical one who needs hands on experience. Well, it wasn't long after I received this revelation that I found myself in Haiti: using the name of Jesus to escape a difficult situation. Let me share this learning experience with you. You see we have a mission work in Port-au-Prince, Haiti, which includes a church and school. We have helped to build the church with our funds and physical labor. The school has developed in the pastor's home next door. We help not only with building but clothing, feeding and caring for those that God has entrusted to our local pastor's care. I took a couple of ladies with me on this mission trip. The goal was quite simple; simple that is if you are a well driller. A well driller I am not but God impressed on me to go and put down a freshwater well on the church property. Our friends in Haiti have never had a fresh drinking water well before so this was to be a real blessing to them and the community of believers.

As we were leaving Miami for the last flight into Port-au-Prince that day, I heard the announcement that our plane would be delayed for one hour. Now that doesn't mean much if you are traveling in a first world country but in a third world country that can spell trouble. It meant that darkness would soon be approaching when we arrived on the island. Feeling a question in my gut, I decided to go for it anyway. My team members were okay with the delay and shortly we landed safely in Haiti. An hour's delay and all our bags lost. That's how we arrived. As many mission trips as I have lead and as much travel as I have done around the world, never have they lost <u>all</u> the bags. Our bags were filled with medical supplies for our people, canned food for use during the trip, and clothes and candy to give to the children at the school. But no bags were to be found. Thankfully one person on the team had packed a couple of changes of clothes in her backpack. Wow, did that ever turn out to be handy! We wore her oversized clothes for several days. Well, back to the airport episode. This seems like a scene from some movie but it happens to be a real life adventure. An adventure of learning on how to use the name that is above all other names. Yes, the name of Jesus is even above the name of fear. Fear is real and it will devour your life just as the word declares, *"your adversary the devil, as a roaring lion, walketh about, seeking whom he may devour"* (1 Peter 5:8). But be encouraged, *" thou (God) hast put all things under his (our) feet"* (Psalm 8:6). ......No bags, it's dark and the airport is closing.

I get in line to declare our bags as lost. I notice it's dark outside and the airport has become empty. A man is quickly walking through yelling in broken English for Pastor Paula. I become excited as I hear my name called out so I let him know that I am still there. You see my interpreter was to wait outside for the team and me. He wa. to hire a tap-tap to shuttle us to the local Inn at which we were scheduled to stay. But Haitians know that darkness is not a friend in Haiti.

There are no streetlights or any lights for that matter. It's just total darkness, pitch dark as we southerners call it. Pitch black, as we say, is when you can put your hand in front of your face and you cannot see it. That's dark! That was Haiti as we were told the airport was closing and we must step outside. I thought we could easily sleep on the floor until daybreak and then maybe our contact would find us, but no! It was outside for us, all on our own. Here we were, white women, no bags, no contact, no ride, and my backpack that I was clutching because it contained the money needed to put down the well. Oh Jesus is all we could say. I told the team to show no fear in their eyes because the enemy will overtake you when you respond in fear to his tricks.

I peaked my head outside the doors and realized no one was there. No begging mass, as is commonplace when we arrive, no tap-taps lined up waiting for hire, no one fighting to carry our luggage, and no one calling out our names in English to welcome us to Haiti. Alone; that is what we were. All alone…. But then the name of Jesus stepped up to bat for us. My prayer was simple: help Jesus!

Now I don't know what your angel looks like. The angel that showed up for me that night was the biggest, black Haitian I have ever seen and his name was Big. Out of the pitch darkness of the night, a man named "Big" came to our rescue. You see, as we stepped out of the safety of the airport, there were men waiting in the darkness with ill intent. Six men surrounded us and there was no help in sight. We began to take authority over the situation in Jesus' name. Suddenly, "Big" steps out of the darkness and says in perfect English, "Do you need help?" Now he is much stronger than all the other men who are all at once talking in Creole. Help? Yes, that was what we needed! Safety was more of what I believed for. "Big" bided us to walk with him. He promised he would get us to safety. He said he would walk us to the police station and there we could stay until a contact was made. It was a short distance that seemed like walking a mile. Surrounded with six men following us, pitch darkness, no interpreter, and no transportation. Stranded!

Before I left the states to make the mission trip to Haiti, the Holy Spirit impressed upon me to take the card that our pastor had given me the last time I was in Port-au-Prince. Little did I know that the reason he gave me the card was because his daughter, who speaks some English, wanted me to have her cell phone number. See the Holy Spirit is always looking out for us when we are not even aware of it. As He prompted me to get the card from the office I gave Him a little trouble by telling Him that I had already left, was on the road and did not want to go back for the card. Now I have learned over the years that the small voice is the one that really speaks the most important whispers. So I repented, turned around, went back for the card and stuck it in my backpack.

Stranded at the police station? Why this was a hole in the wall! Yes. A hewed out cave, that is what it was, not a police station as I imagined! From the smoke filled cave, lit only by a dim bulb, an officer stepped out. Big asked if we might stay there until we could reach someone for help. "Sure, sure" the officer said, but I knew this was going to cost me a considerable financial contribution. I quickly became aware that I would be paying not only Big, but the police, and all the others as well for our safety.

You know they say, white men can't jump but this is one white woman that can. As I was preparing to, how can I say, contribute financially to our safety, I was searching through my bag trying to get money. As I was kneeling down in the police cave, I heard the most eerie voices screeching, "Lady, Lady" and I saw dirt encrusted hands coming from under and over a metal gate. I realized they were prisoners grabbing for the money so they too could pay their way to safety. I made a jump that even scared me. I took off for the street into total darkness again.

What would we do? Where would we go? Deserted by our contact host, surrounded by darkness, and feeling the pinch of dwindling funds. That is what we had. Big asked, "what would we do next?" I said, "Ladies sit down on the ground and let's begin to praise His name." The solution came to us all at the same time. Either the name of Jesus was going to take power over our current situation or we would go under and perish.

We began to praise His name in song. We sang to Jesus and told Him what a strong deliverer He was and how we knew He was going to make a way for us. Just like that I remembered the card in my backpack. I searched through the darkness with my trusty little flashlight and finally found the business card pastor had given me months before. For the first time, I looked on the back of the card. Scribbled, on the back, were two phone numbers I had never seen. Big had a cell phone and I asked him to call the number written by the daughter's name. He agreed and placed the call. Oh, how we could praise the name of Jesus now for we just knew help was on the way. You know what happened? Nothing, no answer! So I said, "let's praise His name some more." We all praised and then I asked Big to try the number the second time. And you know what happened? Nothing.... Well, by this time we felt like Paul and Silas down in a Philippians' jail, long about midnight. Check out Acts 16:25-27 and you will know what I mean. Our spirits never gave up hope even though the circumstances appeared dim. Confidently I asked Big to try the third time. He did. You know what happened? Someone answered! And they could speak broken English. Big was shocked when someone answered and quickly gave the phone to me. My first statement in English was "Come Get Me Now!" The voice responded, "I'll send someone right away." Thank you Jesus," was our reply! Now that was cool enough to build our faith in the name of Jesus but what happened next just left us dazzled by His awesome hand of help. Within a minute or two of hanging up the phone, out of the pitch dark walks up our pastor with the biggest Bible ever under his arm. There was no way he could have gotten there by tap-tap within two minutes or less. How he got there I don't know but I surely was thankful to see him that night. He was greeted by the biggest hugs ever.

At last we safely reached the Inn. We ate and fell into bed with prayers of thanksgiving on our lips. And yes, I have returned many times since this trial by fire. I always call out for "Big" the moment the airport exit doors open. He steps out from among the dense crowd and escorts me to safety. And yes, we drilled the fresh water well, which is still nourishing our friends today.

I know most assuredly that Jesus forever sits at the right hand of the Father, forever interceding for you and me, that's why, " *God also hath highly exalted him, and given him a name which is above every name.*" Not your name or my name but His name....Jesus.

the dance lesson continues......

Chapter 8

Dance Lesson # 5.
SERVATUDE,
"my reasonable service" ……

Servant + Attitude = Servatude….

"Servants, be obedient to them that are your masters according to the flesh, with fear and trembling, in singleness of your heart, as unto Christ; not with eyeservice, as men-pleasers; but as the servants of Christ, doing the will of God from the heart; with good will doing service, as to the Lord, and not to men:" (Ephesians 6:5-7 KJV).

A servant is rendered senseless, released of all self-motivated ambitions, wants and desires. Planted deep, within the very core of the servant's heart is but one fixation and that is to do the will of the one who has mastered the servant's very soul. The fixation is rooted; absorbed in; confined to and controlled by one motivating factor, love. For whatever or whomever the servant loves, the servant will serve. A servant ministers to, waits on, and attends to the passion that is locked up inside his or her own heart. These acts of love produced by the servant solely benefit and please the master who holds the servant's heart.

Thus we find Jesus, the lowly servant, whose heart was filled with pleasing the Father. It was at Capernaum that He revealed His reason for coming when He spoke about the Father's will. In John 6:36 Jesus says, *"For I came down from heaven, not to do mine own will, but the will of him that sent me."* The Father gifted His creation with the life of His only Son, Jesus. The Father's directive for His Son was to let everyone know that the kingdom of God is at hand. He earlier clarified the point in Matthew 6:24, when He said that, *"no man can serve two masters: for either he will hate the one, and love the other; or else he will hold to the one, and despise the other."* Clearly the heart of Jesus could not function separate from the Father's heart. Two beating hearts, with the same rhythm, making one sound. This sound is the sound of love being sent to a dying world that is longing for a savior: Jesus.

The Lord of the Dance has extended his hand and asked for the pleasure of dancing with you. All preparations have been made for the dance. The orchestra is in place, the shining dance floor is spotless, everyone has been adorned with costly apparel, and a fragrant smell of adoration is in the air. Now the time for decision has come. Will you take His hand and surrender to the dance? Will you lean into Him? Can you yield as His breath gently flows across your face? Can you give Him the authority to direct the steps of this waltz? He is the Lord of the Dance, the lover of your soul, the very Christ. yield.....surrender.....give......it's His dance.....

You will not remain the same when the Lord of the Dance makes His presence known in your life. There are times when He gently sweeps in and rearranges the minor details. Then there are the times when He strikes up the band and orchestrates an evening of intimacy where all that you are is consumed in Him. The consuming dance is just that, consuming.

There was a day that I thought I was in control of my own life and destiny. That assumption was short lived as soon as Holy Spirit decided to show up so strong in my life. It was a day like so many others. I was in my home library studying and working on my master's degree in educational leadership. Nothing felt very special about that day. It was just a normal, sunny, Florida day. As I sat at my desk and labored with my studies, the presence of Holy Spirit suddenly invaded the room.

I had always reverentially feared God and tried to live my life in a godly manner. I cannot think of a time that I did not know God. Even in my earliest memories, I have always been keenly aware of His presence in my life. Having avoided many of the pitfalls of adolescents, I never experienced a time in my life where I felt estranged from Him. But this was different. This visitation was not like the others. This visitation came with a hand extending toward me and asking me to dance a dance that I had never experienced before. A dance of total surrender; a dance where the servant's movement flowed only with the master. It was then that Holy Spirit asked me a question that would forever change my life.

You see my life was already changing. My life was not stagnant like a pool with no outlet but in fact it was moving like a gently flowing brook trickling down a mountainside. I trusted God more and more these days. He was astonishing me with answered prayers and my harvest was beginning to come in, or so I thought.

I thought everyone in the college office would pick up on the opportunity. This opportunity to buy stock in an initial public offering was a super chance. That kind of opportunity doesn't come around too often. But no one seemed to take an interest. I had never personally bought stock on the New York Stock Exchange. I really didn't know how or what to do. Something perked up on the inside of me when I heard about the college stock that was going public. It was as if Holy Spirit fine tuned my ears and gave me a desire to learn more. You see, for fourteen years I had been planting financial seed and confessing the Word of God for my dream home. Not just any home, for I had already built, bought and sold homes. But this was going to be my dream home in the guarded, gated community on the golf course. Ahhhh, the home of my dreams with beautiful tile, fancy wallpaper, sunken bathtubs, chandeliers and all the extra trimmings. You know, the cool neighborhood where famous NFL football players and Christian authors all have their homes. A major faith project in the works was what I had.

This faith project was overwhelming to say the least. But I did what every good woman does when she wants something. I pursued like a bulldog on a bone. I was so impressed by Holy Spirit to not let this opportunity pass me by. I was shaking in my boots on the inside but looked like a lion in pursuit of prey on the outside. Holy Spirit would have to guide me on this because I was way out of my league. He likes that you know. He wants to be the Lord of the Dance of our lives. He wants to be in control and have us depend on Him for the very breath we breathe. At this point, without Him, I was breathless!

He gave me a scripture to stand on. A scripture that would produce that which I had been believing for. The moment He spoke Ephesians 3:20 to me I knew I had the bullet that would subdue my prey. It says, *"Now unto him that is able to do exceeding abundantly above all that we ask or think, according to the power that worketh in us."* When He says He *"is able to do,"* that means He is a CAN DO GOD! When He says He is *"exceeding abundantly above,"* that means He is an EXTREME GOD! And when He says *"above all that we ask or think,"* that means He goes BEYOND OUR

CAPACITY! So with my scripture in hand I marched into my banker's office.

While in my banker's office I said only what Holy Spirit lead me to say. My words were something like this. "I desire to buy stock on the Exchange and I want your money to do it with." Stunned was the expression on my banker's face. I followed up by saying, "what have you got to lose? The worst case scenario is that I lose it all and have to pay you back out of my pocket the amount you have loaned me." How could he argue with that logic and the fierceness with which I was pursuing the matter? So with nothing more than my signature I walked out of his office loaded with cash to purchase my stock. What would I do now? When it was all over and I made it back to the car my knees began to shake. But never once did the banker see me sweat!

Now remember, I had Ephesians 3:20 working for me and on my benefit. The Word of God cannot fail nor return void. It **must** perform that which it was sent to do. You and I must learn how to lean into the Word and let it do its work.

Monday arrives and I go to the office of the college and request the paperwork to purchase the stock. The office clerk had to sift through mounds of memos to find the one I was looking for. Her comment was that no one in the entire company, as of yet, had requested the forms for purchase. I was the first one and the only one to her knowledge. I said step back and pass the papers. Let me be the first to fill them out. I was amazed. I was watching God move on my benefit but He required me to follow through on all His instructions. Never did I lean to my own understanding. It was total trust in Him and what He was doing.

I submitted the paperwork to purchase the stock and wrote the check. I left the entire situation in God's hands. Remember now, He was teaching me how to dance. He was teaching me how to lean into Him: how to let Him carry me through life. How to be His handmaiden here on earth so that He alone would get all the glory for what was about to transpire.

It was in His hands now. Would this dream home become a reality? Would I find the dream neighborhood? Would the stock increase in value and be enough to sponsor the dream? Questions that only God could answer.

And answer He did. A couple weeks later, just before daybreak, I once again had a scripture spoken into my spirit by the Holy Ghost. Before He had spoken Ephesians 3:20. This time He was speaking the words, *"this day I have dealt bountifully with you."* It was before dawn that I felt my spirit leap within me so I jumped out of bed and immediately looked up the scripture. It was Psalm 119:17, which says, *"Deal bountifully with thy servant, that I may live, and keep they word."* Wow, another awesome word just for me and my situation. Dancing with Him was becoming the best thing that had ever happened to me. I was learning that God really did know and care about my life and my situation. I was just a little sparrow needing to be clothed and fed and the good master was answering my prayers.

As I was headed to my classroom that morning, I stopped by the library to look at the newspaper and check on the stock listing. To my amazement, just overnight the stock had doubled in value! That was what Holy Spirit was speaking to my spirit in the wee hours of the morning. He had *dealt bountifully* with me! The dream home was now becoming a reality and all because He leaned into me in the dance, and this waltz would produce a lifetime of trust.

The gated community was found. The dream home was built and life was just sweet. And then....as I said before, I was studying in my home library and Holy Spirit walked into the room like a friend coming over for a little fireside chat. He came with a question. He said, ***"Will you give me back all the blessings I have given you?"*** Without one moments hesitation I answered, "yes." My answer was so easy to give because I loved Him so much. He was my everything. I had no need of anyone or anything else because He filled me up. There was no reserved space inside of me that hadn't been touched by Him. And just like that I felt Him satisfied with my answer. Little did I know what that yes would mean.

Within days of my "yes," I graduated with a master's degree in educational leadership. Shortly after that, I received a telephone call where I was asked to come back to my hometown and become the headmaster of a Christian school. I accepted and thought this dance was really taking off. Now the dream home. Would it really be required of me? Oh, I remembered my conversation with Holy Spirit when I told Him that I would give back all the blessings He had blessed me with. After all, I had been allowed to enjoy the dream for four years now. So, the dream would go too but it was a sweet, thankful release. Thankful yes, for allowing me to enjoy the dream those four years.

I was on my way home one afternoon shortly after this. Now I knew that my neighbors had been trying to sell their home for two years but with no takers. So I said to Holy Spirit, "Because this is your dance, are you going to sell the house quickly?" As I pulled into the driveway that day with my eyes wide open I saw a sold sign in the front yard and just knew it was really there. I did a double take. I didn't even have the "For Sale" sign out yet! But I knew that I had prayed and released Holy Spirit to work on my behalf concerning the matter.

I did put the "For Sale" sign on the front lawn. Within days, a couple was driving by on the way to visit their daughter who had just recently bought a home down the street. They so wanted to live close to her because they were now retired and ready to spend time with the grandchildren. There was my dream home that would now become their dream home. It was a cash sale! Homes in that price range did not sell for cash nor did they sell quickly. But when Holy

Spirit wants to dance with you, the details are left up to Him to resolve. And I might add that He takes good care of His business. The only thing He asks of you and me is that we hold the blessings loosely as a good steward would do. Not tight with a stingy, possessive, clinched fist but a gentle watchman's hand that has widely spread fingers.

"Will you give me back all the blessings I have given you?" A dance of total surrender. *"For I came down from heaven, not to do mine own will, but the will of him that sent me."* Jesus, a King who became a servant with God's attitude, rendered senseless, released of all self-motivated ambitions, wants and desires except to do the perfect will of the one that sent Him. Jesus our Servant-King....our model.

the dance lesson continues......

Chapter 9

Dance Lesson # 6.
"BIRTH THE GREATER
LOVE," in me ……

"Thou shalt love the Lord thy God with all thy heart, and with all thy soul, and with all thy mind. This is the first and great commandment. And the second is like unto it, thou shalt love thy neighbor as thyself" (Matthew 22:37-39 KJV).

It would appear that there is a great divide in this passage. One may find it reasonably easy to love the Lord God with all your heart, by putting your emotions into it, and inspiring your intellect to deem Him as worthy of adoration. After all, He is the Lord God of everything and very much desires to have a relationship with you. But now this loving your neighbor as yourself can be quite a bitter pill to swallow. Oh, if one has June Cleaver as a neighbor, then you might find it easy to treat the Beaver as one of your own. But no, The Cleavers have moved out of the neighborhood and the Unlovelys have moved in. Yes, that's right. What Jesus was actually saying in this passage of scripture was to "**love the unlovely**" as you love yourself. Loving the unlovely is like filing your nails with sandpaper….20 grit….coarse….eow!

Now this is a tuff dance lesson. It's more like a Tango than a Waltz. Rough, jerky, dramatic, yet necessary to be more like Him. Why you may even work up a sweat (or glisten as we southern girls say) as you are practicing these steps and movements. But don't give up or give in or give out, you'll make it. When you graduate from this dance lesson, you will be more developed in the greater love, God's pure love. Love that doesn't see the wood beam in another's eye but first checks one's own eye for chips of debris.

Jesus, for the most part, was practical in His teaching style. He didn't draw on elaborate illustrations that the common man could not connect with. Instead He taught using simple relatable stories that inspired the mind to paint pictures. Conversely so, He was able to enamor the most highly educated using thought provoking parables that, at times, pushed them to the point of frustration. And that is where we find Jesus on this day, with the disciples and a challenging lawyer. We find Him teaching a lesson on the greater love: "loving thy neighbor as thyself."

The Bible tells us in Luke chapter 10 that a certain lawyer wanted to know about inheriting eternal life. So he asked Jesus what he needed to do to qualify for it. Jesus replies by asking him, "what does the law say about the matter?" The lawyer responds with the appropriate answer of loving God with your everything and thy neighbor as thyself. Jesus gives him a thumb's up for the proper response and the conversation could have stopped there. But the lawyer wanted to justify himself the Bibles says. So he asks Jesus, "Who is my neighbor?" And the dance lesson begins.....

Jesus renders an unlovely scenario that is deposited in the minds of all those that were listening that day. Unlovely, in the sense that He tells of a certain man who falls into a desperate situation. A desperate situation which seemingly has no positive end in sight. A desperate man because we learn that he has fallen among thieves. It would have been bad enough to simply fall down, but fall down among thieves? That's where the saga begins, for these thieves stripped the man of his clothes, wounded him, and left him half dead. Graphically Jesus reveals the dilemma that had befallen the man. He may have been a "good" man, a respectable man, a prosperous man. He could have even been a famous man of his day. But a thief is a thief. According to John 10:10, *"the thief cometh not but for to steal, and to kill, and to destroy."* The reality is that thieves do steal, they do kill, and they are very destructive. So it is not the reality of thievery that puzzles us about what Jesus is saying, it's what He says next that is the jaw dropper.

It was by happenchance that a priest, a Levite, and a Samaritan passed by the scene of this crime. In today's terminology that would be a preacher, a church elder, and an outcast passed by a man left on the street that had just been mugged. You get the picture.

These thieves took all the man's belongings and threw him in a ditch, bleeding and left for dead. As he was struggling to draw his last breath, while drowning in his own blood, help arrives. Help arrives but does not stop. Jesus tells us that a priest who is capable of helping looked from a distance and saw the situation. It appeared a little too messy for him to get involved in so he chose to slip to the other side of the road. Quickly he was on his way, away from the one in need. Within seconds a second passerby spots the same situation just ahead. This man is a Levite who tends to the altar in the House of the Lord. He is familiar with helping because that is what he does. He helps keep the Temple in order and the sacrifice of praise forever before the Lord. But he too chooses to leave the man in the ditch but only after going over and taking a look-see at the man. Then a Samaritan journeyed by. This man, the Samaritan, was not a priest who was chosen by God to stand in the gap for the people. Neither was he an altar worker who was familiar with

God's required procedures of service. He was in fact just a mixed breed who was rejected from society. What further set him apart from the holy man and the temple worker was that when he saw the man in the ditch, he had compassion on him and chose to NOT leave him there. The others were strong enough, capable enough, but not willing enough to do something about the situation. This Samaritan was compassionate enough to reach out a helping hand to this man in his suffering, desperate situation. This "good" man not only identifies with the one lying in the ditch, beat up, and robbed by thieves, but he gets in the ditch with him, binds up his wounds, by pouring in oil and wine, picks him up and sets him on his own beast and carries him to the Inn. While at the Inn, he nourishes him and pays the bill in advance. What the thieves left for dead has now been restored to life.

Speechless the lawyer stands looking at Jesus. Jesus summarizes his case at hand by asking the lawyer, " which of the three do you think was a neighbor to the one that fell among the thieves?" The lawyer yields the floor by surmising that "the one who showed mercy on him" was indeed his neighbor. Jesus confirms that he has gotten it right and challenges him to go and do likewise.

An "unlovely situation" that requires a greater love. Not just a situation that we can "deal" with. But situations that go beyond all natural love capabilities. Situations that stretch love boundaries to the maximum and then start to pull you way beyond the place you thought you would be able to stretch to.

That's the greater love, the love for the unlovely.

It took several years for me to be able to dance to this rhythm. I was like the nerd on the dance floor with two left feet when it came to the greater love. So Jesus, as wonderful as He is, allowed me to experience life helping unlovelys out of the ditch. He truly loved me so much that He wanted to birth His greater love for all humanity in me.

Human nature is to care for its own. We simply are creatures of habit. We like our small circle of family and friends that are most like us. We fellowship with those that enjoy the restaurants we chose, like to shop at our favorite stores, and most likely attend the church we attend. But what about that one irritating person who doesn't fit into any area of your life? That is the one we tend to avoid. Oh, we say we love them when we are in church but the parking lot is a different story. You know, they (Mr. and Mrs. Unlovely) are the ones that cram their car door into yours, nicking the paint, and neeeever say sorry. Or they run ahead of you in the rain to get to the church door first and then let it close in your face just as you are arriving with a screaming kid in each arm. Yeah....those are the people I'm talking about, the unlovely ones. Now maybe, just maybe, it wouldn't be so very bad if you had time to go pray and repent, and make amends for what you were thinking about the unlovely people. But what happens when you are the one who has to go to the platform because you are supposed to address the congregation in the next ten minutes! Bummer.....earthly......self-seeking...... conditional love......not Christ-like.

Such an extraordinary model of unconditional love; Jesus, the greater lover. They lead Him away to the hill of the skull, Golgotha. With nails they pierced His hands and feet. Upon His head a crown of thorns was placed. The flesh on His back lay gapping open after being beaten with thirty-nine stripes. Openly wounded, that was the master as He hung on the cross that day. Spit upon, ridiculed and mocked as they positioned the sign "King of the Jews" above His head. Yet characterized as a total surrender to the Father's great redemptive plan. What great love, this love that Jesus had for the world. Love for the unlovelys, you and me. A life given to unconditional love that He summed up so well in His own words when He uttered, *"Father, forgive them; for they know not what they do"* (Luke 23:34). Jesus truly is our model of love stretched beyond known boundaries as He walked the extra mile and gave His coat too.

"Greater love hath no man than this, that a man lay down his life for his friends" (John 15:13).

So you see, it really doesn't matter if the Cleaver's live next-door or the Munster's. It's really all about a heart thing. The world dances with its own and is *"drunken with the blood of the saints, and with the blood of the martyrs of Jesus,"* (Revelation 17:6). You and I, as believers, dance to the song of the Spirit that whistles over us........ come.

the dance lesson continues......

Chapter 10

Dance Lesson # 7.
MY SPOKEN WORD,
"my heart's confession" ......

"The word is nigh thee, even in thy mouth, and in thy heart: that is, the word of faith, which we preach; (Romans 10:8 KJV).

"You must '**believe the Word**' with your mind, '**hope in the Word**' with your heart, and '**expect the Word**' to manifest with your spirit. During the middle of the night, aroused from my sleep, those were the exact words I heard Holy Spirit speak to my spirit.

Your mind, your heart, and your spirit must believe, hope, and expect the Word of God to go and perform that which it is sent to do. It is worth noting that the mouth will reveal the status and content of all three of these parts of any human being.

This is a vital dance lesson that must be mastered. For you see, this lesson repeats itself every waking moment of consciousness. It connects the mind, the heart and spirit to the mouth. The mouth that cannot hide the intent of the heart, mind, or spirit: no matter how hard it tries. It just tells the whole story without leaving anything to the imagination. I have heard it said that practice makes perfect; and truly practice is what it takes to get the mouth to speak as God speaks.

Jesus is the Word of God as stated by John in chapter one verse fourteen. *"And the Word was made flesh, and dwelt among us."* Jesus, the Word, pulled from our Father God, wrapped in human flesh that lived, taught, and walked with us. The Word of God living among us, how awesome is that! My mind cannot contain or even begin wrap around that statement.

Let's watch the Word, Jesus, in action.

Jesus has just made His triumphal entry into Jerusalem. It was now evening and He and the disciples go over to Bethany to rest. The next morning He is returning, with the disciples, to Jerusalem and is hungry for breakfast. Some distance ahead He spots a tree. It is bearing leaves so He presumes it is also fruitful. When He reaches the tree and lifts the leaves: He is dissatisfied when He finds no fruit or figs.

Now we see the "God-talk" in action.

Jesus understood what the tree was saying because the Bible tells us that He <u>answered</u> the tree. He answered the tree? Yes. See the "fruitless tree" can be any and all situations, circumstances, or life-hurdles that you and I may encounter. Whether small or large, sometimes or daily, bothersome or earth shaking: they are hurdles to jump over or go around.

A tree, speaking fruitlessness to the creator of the universe, how foolishly bold! For Hebrews 11:3 reminds us that, *"we understand that the worlds were framed by the word of God."* A tree speaking negative productivity to Jesus? Who do you think will come out blessed in this situation? Jesus cannot fail, so I guess it will not be the tree. And the tree it was not.

"No man eat fruit of thee hereafter for ever," were the exact words **spoken** to the tree that day by Jesus. The disciples overheard what was going on. Little did they know that a teachable moment was on the horizon.

The next morning they passed by the same fig tree, which the day before was green, waving leaves of the coming harvest. Peter, God love him, pipes up and brings the tree to the Master's attention. Why? Because now the once thriving tree had withered up from the roots, overnight. Astonishing! As Peter points out the change of events, Jesus uses "with-it-ness" to seize the moment and once again continues to expand on the Kingdom's method of operation.

Jesus clearly details, for the disciples, how powerful spoken words are when they are expelled from the heart. He speaks these words that remain alive today. *"For verily I say unto you, That whosoever shall say unto this mountain, Be thou removed, and be thou cast into the sea; and shall not doubt in his heart, but shall believe that those things which he saith shall come to pass; he shall have whatsoever he saith"* (Mark 11:23).

The withered tree was all the evidence needed to prove the case in point. Your spoken words of life or death are a spiritual weapon that no enemy can defeat. *"Death and life are in the power of the tongue: and they that love it shall eat the fruit thereof"* (Proverbs 18:21).

So are our spoken words, the confession of our hearts, the thoughts of our mind, really that important? Let's once again visit the scripture we started this dance lesson with. This time we look at chapter 10:9-10 as Apostle Paul writes to the Romans. His words are, *"That if thou shalt **confess** with thy mouth the Lord Jesus, and shalt believe in thine heart that God hath raised him from the dead, thou shalt be saved, for with the heart man believeth unto righteousness; and **with the mouth confession** is made unto salvation."* Clearly our spoken words are very important. So important in fact that the Apostle Paul states they are audibly required for our salvation. Now that's important and powerful!

The heart plus the mind plus the mouth equals the life that I live. Defeated or victorious? I choose which life I will live by the words that I speak. *"But the word is very nigh unto thee, in thy mouth, and in thy heart, that thou mayest do it. I have set before you life and death, blessing and cursing: therefore choose life, that both thou and thy seed may live:"* (Deuteronomy 30:14,19).

The Word of God speaks blessings over us. Daily we must allow the Word to wash over us. Psychologists tell us that the mind can have a repetitive thought 600 times in a single day. A simple example of this is could be when we hear a snappy little tune that is attached to happiness. Right now I am thinking of a commercial I use to hear as a kid. There was this jingle for bandages. It went like this: I am stuck on Band-Aid brand cause Band-Aids stuck on me! (Now try and get that out of your mind the rest of the day after reading this.) I could hear that commercial and hum it the rest of the day. That is a repetitive thought that produces, in this case, happiness. It is attached to my happy childhood memories. In fact, I would enjoy using all the bandages in the box, all at once, even when they were not needed. That was just fun! I loved peeling the band-aid from the wrapper and sticking it anywhere, even on the dog. Funny huh? Yes, but with a true Biblical principle in motion. As my mind, from the heart, would sing through my mouth this little jingle, I would feel great, enthusiastic and happy as I bandaged everyone in sight. The same is true of the spoken Word of God. When spoken words come from a heart and mind that has stayed fixed on the Word, and believes that the words spoken will come to pass, then, situations and circumstances are required to line up with God's unchanging words of life. So, dance to the lesson because...... it's just like that.

the dance lesson continues......

Chapter 11

Dance Lesson # 8.
PRAYER AND FASTING,
"the place of intimacy, a quiet devotion, open power and authority" ......

"But thou, when thou fastest, anoint thine head, and wash thy face; That thou appear not unto men to fast, but unto thy Father which is in secret: and thy Father, which seeth in secret, shall reward thee openly" ~ Jesus (Matthew 6:17-18).

"And he withdrew himself into the wilderness, and prayed" (Luke 5:16).

The music softens, the people recede, and the lights dim as silence falls over the dance floor. You grope in the darkness for the master's hand. Slowly, gently, He rescues you from the abandonment. And you free fall into His loving arms once again. For you have just entered, the secret place. A place where no one can dance for you. An alone place. The master and you, together, dancing in the secret pavilion of our Lord. His secret place of habitation. *"He shall cover thee with his feathers, and under his wings shall thou trust:" (Psalm 91:4).*

I am sure you have heard that, "fasting and prayer draws one closer to God." I disagree somewhat with that statement. God has not moved, nor has His voice weakened. His Word still speaks and He is forever on His Throne. What **does** happen, when we begin to withdraw into a life style of fasting coupled with prayer, is that His voice and actions begin to be <u>noticed</u> and <u>received</u> by us. His voice always speaks to us. His actions are always manifesting towards us. We just haven't focused and slowed down enough to be able to hear what He has said or see what He has done on our behalf. Fasting and prayer draws us into the secret place of the Most High where we can live in the shadow of the Almighty, (see Psalm 91).

Fasting takes away natural food and supplies us with spiritual revelation. Just as prayer takes away mindless words spoken and replaces dialogue with meaningful conversation.

This dance lesson requires the endurance of a well-trained athlete and the devotion of a mother who cares for her only child. Taking food away from self and replacing it with time spent in prayer is the task at hand. Easy to say.... difficult to achieve....accomplished only when you are nestled safely in Him.

This giving up of needed food and talking with the Lord produces marked results. Let's look at the Biblical account of King Jehoshaphat in II Chronicles 20. Please allow me to paraphrase this story for you.

Up until this point, King Jehoshaphat had prospered greatly because he had followed the Lord's ways. He makes a great slip up by developing an affinity or agreement with the evil King Ahab. He agrees to fight with and for him if King Ahab will return the favor. This agreement sore displeases the Lord. The Bible declares that after this, a great multitude rose against Judah which caused Jehoshaphat to fear exceedingly. So to get the attention of God, King Jehoshaphat calls a fast throughout all the land.

Judah, or the praise team, as we like to call them, fasted and gathered themselves together to ask help of the Lord. They pushed back from the table and spent time in prayer. King Jehoshaphat starts off the prayer meeting by reminding God of how great He is and how weak they are against the enemy. He then makes this statement to God which defines what fasting and prayer truly is. He says, *"our eyes are upon thee" (II Chronicles 20:12).*

"Our eyes are upon thee".......that is the summation of what fasting and prayer is all about. No longer are our eyes on our own difficult circumstances but they are upon the living God who is able to deliver us out of or carry us through all the attacks of the enemy!

As the inhabitants of Judah humbled themselves, the Spirit of the Lord came in their midst and declared, *"Be not afraid nor dismayed by reason of this great multitude; for the battle is not yours but God's, (II Chronicles 20:15).* In verse 16 the Spirit gives directions on how to win without fighting. *"Ye shall not need to fight in this battle;* **set** *yourselves,* **stand** *ye still, and* **see** *the salvation of the Lord with you,"* *(emphasis added).* Set, meaning to "position yourself".... stand, meaning to not "get anxious".......and see or watch God "show up" strong every time to win the battle for you.

V-I-C-T-O-R-Y....was produced when the people gave up life-sustaining food and the most valuable commodity they had.......time which they spent in prayer.

God's plan worked for Israel and His powerful tool of fasting and prayer still works today. This plan, God's plan, takes the focus away from all distractions and noise of life and allows us to lean into Him and feel the strength of His canopy over us.

The "noise" of life is filtered out when we are positioned (through prayer and fasting) safely in the master's hands. As we rest in Him, our heart begins to repeat a silent prayer. "My eyes are upon you........my eyes are upon you." And as our eyes are fixed upon Him, the answers we were seeking for are revealed. *"Ask, and it shall be given you; seek and ye shall find; knock, and it shall be opened unto you" (Matthew 6:7).* So we position ourselves in Him, stand the test of time, and watch God show up strong on our behalf, every single time.

Canopied in a place where no one can dance for you. An intimate place. Just the master and you, together, dancing in the secret pavilion of our Lord as you focus all adoration on Him.......Set......Stand......See......

"And when Jehoshaphat and his people came to take away the spoil of them, they found among them in abundance both riches with the dead bodies, and precious jewels, which they stripped off for themselves, more than they could carry away: and they were three days in gathering of the spoil, it was so much" (II Chronicles 20:25).

"the place of intimacy, a quiet devotion, open power and authority" ......

the dance lesson continues......

71

Chapter 12

Dance Lesson # 9.
BIND AND LOOSE,
"the breaker anointing" ......

"And I will give unto thee the keys of the kingdom of heaven: and whatsoever thou shalt bind on earth shall be bound in heaven: and whatsoever thou shalt loose on earth shall be loosed in heaven" (Matthew 16:19).

That's the power of agreement! Heaven agreeing with earth. God agreeing with your spoken words and actions.

King David knew this "breaker anointing" well. He was such a warrior yet a lover. He could shed blood during a battle and then pen words of love to his God. Because of this anointing, he never ran from the roar of the enemy.

It was just after David had been anointed for the third time that the Philistines began to spread themselves in the valley of Rephaim. Now David was King over Judah and Israel, a united kingdom.

The warrior King went down to take a look at the enemy and the enemy went down to take a look at the King. The Bible declares that, *"the Lord God of hosts was with him."* As he began to inquire of the Lord, David asked God, *"Shall*

I go up to the Philistines? Wilt thou deliver them into mine hand? And the Lord said unto David, Go up: for I will doubtless deliver the Philistines into thine hand" (II Samuel 5:19). With the Word of the Lord on his side, David went down to the enemy's camp and smote them. As David finished off the Philistines he said, *"the Lord hath broken forth upon mine enemies before me, as the breach of waters"* (II Samuel 5:20). He then names the place, Baelperazim because the Lord had demonstrated His power when He broke the enemy's stronghold.

The "breaker anointing" was not only for the warrior King David. It is available to you and me today. When we find ourselves in a battle with the enemy, we must follow David's lead and allow God to fight for us. Our natural strength is too frail to combat the adversary. God's anointing brings wisdom, courage, and strength to defeat any opponent.

Today many believers are living a defeated life. We, as believers, must realize that, *"we wrestle not against flesh and blood, but against principalities, against powers, against the rulers of the darkness of this world, against spiritual wickedness in high places"* (Ephesians 6:12).

While in Haiti preparing to drill a well, I met with some powers of darkness. Assigned rulers of darkness that have been in control of the region for a long time. Darkness that did not want God's people to come in and supply fresh drinking water for the believers. Darkness that wanted to keep the people in poverty, lack, and sickness.

From the beginning this was a difficult mission's trip. It became even more difficult when we started to drill the water well to help relieve God's people of sickness due to drinking contaminated water.

Our time was limited to one week for this trip to Haiti. It seemed as if no one would cooperate with us. To begin with, only women (who knew nothing about drilling wells) wanted to go on the trip. When we arrived, we could not find a company to put down the well for a reasonable price. After hitting brick wall after brick wall, I finally had had enough. I knew the price God told me to pay for the well. He had supplied all the money for it and I was not about to pay more than He said or sent. I knew that He had sent just the right people on the trip because He does all things well. It was not weakness on God's part that was causing all the delays; it was the adversary that was throwing all this junk at us so that we would go home defeated. But I refused to bring back an "evil report" saying there were too many giants in the land and we were as grasshoppers in our own eyes. I did like David, I inquired of the Lord.

That night I said, " Ladies let's pray." As we began to pray in the Spirit, I saw my hands tied with a cord, bound. We interceded for just a few minutes and I felt a shift in the atmosphere as we moved past "the war or wrestling" of the second heavens and moved into the third heaven where it's just.......easy, you know, the "glory realm."

With ease we fell asleep.

While at breakfast the next morning, the cell phone rang. My interpreter started by saying, "Pastor Paula, you know".... and I stopped him. I said, "No, let me tell you before you say anything. I am going to get the well drilled and for the exact price God told me." With a dropped jaw he asked how did I know that? I began to tell him about the prayer on the night before when I felt the shift in the atmosphere and the "breaker anointing" that came into the situation and changed everything for our good.

The anointing is the unchanging, all-powerful, timeless anointing. We must tap into all that God has for us. We must refuse to live a lack-luster life that just sits on a shelf and collects dust.

Waltzing with the strong warrior King is far better and more satisfying than wrestling with the devil. *"The blessing*

of the Lord, it maketh rich and he addeth no sorrow with it"
(Proverbs 10:22).

the dance lesson continues……

Chapter 13

Dance Lesson # 10.
SEEDTIME AND HARVEST,
"your covenant promise" ......

"While the earth remaineth, seedtime and harvest, and cold and heat, and summer and winter, and day and night shall not cease" (Genesis 8:22).

Who would have believed that this simple southern girl, from nowhere's Ville, would one day be sitting, on a sofa, in the home of one of God's greatest "Generals of Faith?" God's General, Dr. Oral Roberts.

Why I was a crybaby! I couldn't help it. As soon as I drove up on the property, started heading for the door, the tears began to flow. I was moved deep in my spirit because of the magnitude of the moment. "God's General of Faith?" I thought only people like Benny Hinn, Rod Parsley, or Bill Johnson would be allowed to sit at Dr. Roberts' feet and receive a blessing of impartation. But not me! Well, yes me! When you have been asked to waltz with the Master, you never know where it is that He is going to lead. There I was, a handmaiden, dancing with an awesome God. And it can happen for you too!

I recall that day vividly. I still thank God that He allowed me to sit with His General, Dr. Oral Roberts just three months before he was promoted to Glory. How awesome it was to listen as he taught on "seed-faith." I was forever changed as he laid his hands on me, spoke a blessing, and came into agreement with me for "fullness of ministry."

You see it was because of the ministry of Dr. Oral Roberts that my family knew about "seed-faith." My Granny always watched his programs, read his books, and supported his ministry. For many, many years she sent a widow's portion to help hold his hands up. I can still hear him say, "God is your source, so give, and expect a miracle." And how true that is!

Everything under the sun has a definite place of beginning. The beginning place of everything is a seed. The seed is the source of the new life that is to come.

As an elementary classroom teacher, the students and I always had great fun with our science lessons. We were especially excited about growing our own little garden. Our little garden simply amounted to paper cups filled with soil that were placed on the windowsill. But that was all right because from that little seed in a cup, a harvest was produced.

Now it didn't start out as a bumper crop. On the contrary, it started out as a bean in a bag! Teachers are very resourceful and this science experiment was no exception.

The students and I pooled our resources and came up with the necessary tools to be a farmer for a day. We got our sandwich bags, a brown paper towel, some water, a shoebox and found a dark spot to put all the "necessaries" in. Each student got a bean, placed it on a wet paper towel and zipped it up in a plastic bag. Then we stacked all the bags in a shoebox and put it in a dark corner......and waited...... with expectation.

It's amazing what happens when you leave the seed in the soil. Why in just a few short days, our bean began to "germinate." As it germinated it sprouted a root. As soon as the root was showing we transplanted it to a paper cup filled with potting soil. And there we left it on the windowsill. With the right amount of water and sunshine, the root began to grow down deep into the soil and a "seedling" began to burst out of the top of the soil as it reached for the sunshine.

Each seed has a designated number of days till germination. Every seedling has a designated number of days until it grows into a plant. And every plant has a designated number of days until it is developed enough to produce a crop or harvest.

When the fullness of the crop comes, it is then time to gather the abundance of the harvest.

The same is true with our faith. Our faith is alive. When we plant a seed of faith in quality soil, an expected harvest is sure to come. Why even a second grader can say amen to that.

In the Bible, the Apostle Paul wrote about the "seed science experiment" to the Corinthians. He was a great teacher. This is what it sounded like in Paul's classroom the day he taught on seedtime and harvest. He sums up the principle so well by saying, *"But this I say, He which soweth sparingly shall reap sparingly; and he which soweth bountifully shall reap also bountifully. Every man according as he purposeth in his heart, so let him give; not grudgingly, or of necessity: for God loveth a cheerful giver, and God is able to make all grace abound toward you; that ye, always having all sufficiency in all things, may abound to every good work: Now he that ministereth seed to the sower both minister bread for your food, and multiply your seed sown, and increase the fruits of your righteouness; Being enriched in every thing to all bountifulness, which causeth through us thanksgiving to God. (II Corinthians 9:6-8, 10-11).*

I believe you and I are the bountiful sowers that Apostle Paul was referring to and our harvest of bounty is just about ripe for the gathering.

Many seeds have been sown into my life through these dancing lessons with the King. I desire for my life to produce a bumper crop for the Kingdom of God. I want to be the quality soil in which the seed has been planted. I expect to reap a soul-winner's harvest blessing to cast at His feet and hear Him say, "Well done, good and faithful servant, enter into your rest."

I am thankful that God set me up and allowed me to glean from the master teacher of Seed-Faith, Dr. Oral Roberts.

And as this dance lesson began to draw to a close....

the King paused, and the music began to change......

Wrap Up

Webster's Dictionary defines dancing as moving with measured steps or to move rhythmically. The waltz is described as a ballroom dance in three-four time, or simply to skip about with joy. I define "waltzing" as the day I said, "yes" to the Lord of the Dance. It has been so very exciting these years since He asked me to dance. And I shall never stop dancing with Him.......I promise......

I have had so much fun with this project given to me by Holy Spirit. Now that it is complete, I am already anticipating what's coming next. Maybe it will have something to do with being...... *loosed in the glory*.....how glorious is that-cool Jesus!

The Great Invitation

You may have read this book about my "dancing lessons" with the King and not know Him. Or, you may
know Him but just haven't danced with Him lately. Either
way, I would like to pray with you. I would like to introduce
you to the King of all Kings, Jesus, my Lord and Savior.
If you would like to receive Him as your Lord and Savior
please pray this prayer with me now.....

Jesus, I am a sinner. Please forgive me of all the things
I've done wrong. I believe you are the Son of God, that you
were crucified, buried, and you arose. Wash me now in your
precious blood and make me white as snow. I love you Jesus
and I will live for you. Guide my life for I am now in your
hands. Amen.

For those that have not danced with the King lately, the
relationship is right where you left it. He is waiting for you
just as you are. Lean into Him and let Him restore your joy
of salvation. Pray with me now. Dear Jesus, I am sorry I have
neglected our life together. I want to know you passionately
as before. Renew a right spirit within me so that I may live
for you. I love you Jesus. Amen.

If you would like to be filled with the Spirit, it's as simple
as asking Holy Spirit to come in. He is such a gentlemen that
He waits for you to invite Him in. When asked, He will come
in and fill you to overflowing with joy and power. Let's ask

Him to come in now. Please pray with me. Holy Spirit please come into my heart and fill me to overflowing with your joy and power. I receive you into my life now. Amen.

You are now in for the best time of your life, whether you just received salvation, renewed your relationship with Him or asked to be filled with the Holy Spirit. Jesus is the best friend, Lord and Savior anyone could ever have and the Holy Spirit will teach you all things. Welcome to God's family. He loves you and I do too!

Please write and tell me about your commitment or renewal to Christ, and your infilling of the Holy Spirit today. There is power in your testimony! I want to hear from you.

About the Author

Paula Douglas holds an earned Bachelor of Science degree, and a Master's of Educational Leadership degree. She has also been awarded a Doctorate of Divinity. By trade, she is a schoolteacher and principal. She spent twenty years teaching in the public schools of Duval County, Florida. By calling, she is a pastor with a passionate desire for missions. Her on fire church, which was founded by her parents, The Reverends Paul and Merie Douglas, is located in Hemingway, SC just inland of Myrtle Beach.

**I would love to hear from you.
Please contact me at:**

Paula Douglas Ministries
Door of Faith Church – Media Outreach
P.O. Box 607
Hemingway, SC 29554
843.558.1592
www.pauladouglas.org

LaVergne, TN USA
24 May 2010
183836LV00001B/11/P